A Healthy G
to Sport

Dedication

This book simply wouldn't have happened without the amazing support of a few people.

My wife Sharon is the ultimate role model, editor, wife and mom!

My parents, Ron and Mary Mackinnon, provided me with so many incredible sporting and life opportunities that have shaped my life.

My in-laws, Val and Ian Adamson, have been ever-encouraging.

Thomas Stengel, from Meyer and Meyer Publishing, has been incredibly patient with me over the year this book took to develop, and has provided a magic touch that has got this book to print.

Finally, I have to thank my three amazing children, Chelsea, Sean and Ian, who make it all so worthwhile.

Ironman Edition

A Healthy Guide to Sport

IronKids™

How to Make Your Kids Healthy, Happy and Ready to Go

By Kevin Mackinnon

Published by Meyer & Meyer Sport

IRONKIDS is a registered trademark of Sara Lee Bakery Group, used here by permission

British Library Cataloguing in Publication Data
A catalogue record for this book is available from the British Library

Mackinnon, Kevin:
A Healthy Guide to Sport
Ironkids
Oxford: Meyer & Meyer Sport (UK) Ltd., 2005
ISBN 1-84126-106-8

© 2005 by Meyer & Meyer Sport (UK) Ltd.
Aachen, Adelaide, Auckland, Budapest, Graz, Johannesburg,
New York, Olten (CH), Oxford, Singapore, Toronto
Member of the World
Sports Publishers' Association (WSPA)
www.w-s-p-a.org
Printed and bound by: FINIDR, s. r. o.,Český Těšín
ISBN 1-84126-106-8
E-Mail: verlag@m-m-sports.com
www.m-m-sports.com

Contents

Introduction

Children in today's society are in trouble. In Canada, 34 percent of our children are considered clinically obese. The average child in North America spends about 28 hours watching television or playing computer games every week. (Yes, that's four hours a day!)

Those kids are growing up to become obese adults. Many of them aren't even making it to adulthood without serious health problems—Type 2 diabetes, a disease that affects overweight children, has become so common that many health professionals feel it has reached epidemic proportions here in North America.

At one end of the sporting spectrum, we have many children who are so inactive they are getting sick. At the other end, we have a group of children being pushed into sports and are doing too much, too soon.

Children should pursue a variety of sports while growing up. One of the worst things we can do as parents is force our children to specialize too soon—7-year-old children shouldn't have to give up every other sport to focus on their hockey careers!

It's important to remember that our children aren't going to become great athletes just because we want them to. As Dan and Jay Bielsma pointed out in their book, "So Your Son Wants to Play in the NHL," children "make it" in sports not because of what their parents do for them—great athletes become the best at what they do because of their own inner drive to succeed.

This book is not going to give you a blueprint to turn little Johnny or Susie into a professional triathlete. The goal is to provide a comprehensive plan that will help parents guide their children toward a healthy love of sports. This book will show parents, and kids, how to get involved in triathlon and other "lifestyle" sports that they will be able to do for the rest of their lives.

Triathlon is a fantastic endeavor for children because it promotes involvement in three "lifestyle" sports: swimming, biking and running. No matter what the age, children who develop some skills in these sports will be able to pursue any sport they would like when they are older.

Sport should be the most enjoyable, and educational, activity our children get to do. It should provide them with a positive feeling about themselves. It should teach them that they can improve themselves in all endeavors of life by working hard and persevering. It should teach them about the benefits of working as part of a team or training group.

It should show them how much they gain in life by striving to achieve their goals. It should help them become good people.

I hope this book will help both parents and children learn to love being active.

Section 1: The Basics

Creating a Fun Environment

I seem to meet two different types of people in my life—people who remember gym class with fond memories and those who hated every minute of it.

I'm one of the ones who loved going to gym. More than often, gym class simply involved being split up into two teams and playing some sort of a game. The natural athletes

in the group took over, while those who weren't so sports-inclined were pretty much left out of the action for most of the class.

So, while gym class was fun for me, it wasn't for so many of the kids I grew up with.

Many sports programs for kids run the same way. Five-year-olds in Canada are thrown onto the ice in full hockey equipment after one or two practices and told to play a game. There are always a couple of "natural" players who dominate the action, while the rest of the players spend most of their time watching, not playing. I noticed a similar trend in the soccer programs my children have been involved in.

Those same sports programs typically try to emphasize the concept of participation—everyone gets equal time on the ice or on the field. What they're missing, though, is the concept of equal opportunity. The natural athletes touch the puck or soccer ball almost all the time, while children who could be good players—if they had some training—are left as spectators even as they are supposed to be playing.

Find a Program with the Right Attitude

So how do we avoid getting our children involved in a program in which they won't have a chance to truly participate? The first thing to do is to find a program that will provide a lot of positive feedback. The program needs to be fun too! For most kids, that means the program needs to provide lots of games that ensure everyone gets to play, and everyone has a good time. While providing all of that, the program must also emphasize skill development.

A Positive Environment

As a fitness consultant, I'm not allowed to have a bad day. When I arrive for a training session with a club or to do a workout with a client, they are expecting me to be enthusiastic and positive. I have to provide constructive criticism of their technique and make their training experience both worthwhile and enjoyable.

Being positive while coaching was drilled into me when I first started coaching tennis. As a teenager, I started working at a tennis camp in Vermont, where the camp director, Ted Hoehn, was obsessed with creating a positive attitude on the court.

During our coaching evaluations, Ted used to sit behind the court with a chart and would count the positive and negative statements we made to the children while we were coaching.

"For every negative thing you say, you need to provide four positives," Ted would always tell us.

Let me tell you, with some of the kids, coming up with that third and fourth positive statement was tough, but with a bit of imaginative thinking, it could be done.

When it comes to finding a sports program for your kids, you need to find one that follows Ted's basic premise ... there needs to be much more of an emphasis on positive feedback.

When you're evaluating a program, you don't have to ask the coaches how many positive versus negative statements they intend to say to your children, but you do want to see how they run the program. Does the coach look for the good things the children are doing, and emphasize those? Are the kids having fun? Do they look forward to going to practice?

Look For an "All-Inclusive" Approach

One of the things that attracted me to the sport of triathlon almost 20 years ago was the fact that it was an "all-inclusive" sport. Here was an activity that everyone could be involved in. Everyone could feel good about doing an event or training for one. Everyone got pretty much the same benefits from being involved—and every competitor in the event was a "winner" because they finished.

Children who aren't natural athletes who end up watching others succeed on a hockey rink or a soccer field aren't having fun. They don't feel like winners, even if their team wins, because they haven't contributed to that victory. When they finish a triathlon, though, they know they are winners because it was their efforts that got them across the finish line. Winning is fun, which is why its important for parents to introduce their children to sports activities in which they can "win" from day one.

In their book "So Your Son Wants to Play in the NHL," Dan and Jay Bielsma talk about the time Dan complained to his father about one of the weaker players on the team. His dad told him to be careful because one day he might be in a position where he was one of the weaker players on a team.

Those words came back to haunt Dan during his first NHL game for the Los Angeles Kings when he found himself playing next to Wayne Gretzky, arguably the greatest hockey player the world has ever seen.

Rather than complain about the "rookie" that he had to play with, Gretzky was the first to welcome Dan to the team—a sign of a truly great athlete. By helping Dan feel more comfortable, Gretzky was helping himself, and his team.

There should be no "prima donnas" in a sports program. Everyone should be taken seriously and treated with respect. An "all-inclusive" sports program celebrates everyone's achievements. Making a good pass during a game helps the team succeed. In individual sports, just finishing a race or a practice is a great achievement. Coaches, athletes and parents should celebrate a finish that happens in a personal best time.

Make Sure it's Fun

A positive coaching environment is one thing, but children won't want to be involved in a sports program unless it's fun.

The gym at George R. Allan Elementary School in Hamilton is tiny, but somehow on Thursday afternoons, my wife and I manage to get more than 60 children between the ages of 5 and 10 years old running, jumping, and throwing for a half hour.

When we can, we do get outside, but Canada's cold and snowy winters make that impossible for three or four months every year.

So we do it all inside, in the gym. It works because the kids come for that half hour and have fun. Most of what they're doing is playing games, while also developing skills that will help their cardiovascular fitness, balance, speed, flexability, and strength, which will someday help them excel in any sport they might want to pursue.

The trick is to have the children work on those skills while playing games. I know I've coached a good practice when the kids finish the day talking about how much fun they've had and how many different games they got to play. When they don't realize that along the way they had been working hard on various skills, I know I did a good job!

Later in the book, we'll look at some games that will help develop skills.

For Younger Children, Look for Programs that are Less "Sport Specific"

The program we run on those Thursday afternoons might be called "The Running Club," but the real goal is to provide a general program that will help the kids develop universal sport skills.

As parents, we have to face the reality that our children aren't ready to decide what their sporting passion is going to be when they're 5 years old. I was 10 when I started playing tennis, 15 when I started running, and 22 when I became a professional triathlete.

Finding programs like the one my wife and I have developed is tough. There are very few "general" sports programs for kids.

In Canada, we can put 3-year-olds in hockey programs that teach them little more than hockey skills, but finding a program that will develop running, jumping, throwing and strength skills is difficult.

One of the best sports I've come across for developing some general skills is gymnastics. "Kindergym" programs typically emphasize a lot of balance and jumping skills, which are an excellent way for children to start being active.

If you can't find a "general" sports program or a good gymnastics session in your area, get together with some other parents, follow some of the principles from this book, and start one yourself!

Skill Development Is Where it's at!

I've mentioned a few times how we all like to win. The thing is, though, if you can't do a sport properly, you're never going to have an opportunity to win.

For kids, winning can mean simply doing something better than they were able to do it before. In other words, skill development can be very satisfying for children, if it's presented to them in the right way. Learning to shoot a basketball properly is very exciting for a child. The same feeling of achievement can be attained when a child learns to long jump with more skill so they can go farther. Learning to swim with better technique will allow a child to not only swim faster, they will be able to go farther, too, providing yet another sense of achievement.

Many parents aren't willing to accept that a sense of "winning" can come in the form of doing something better. When I'm coaching younger children, I often hear from the parents that the kids "want to play more games" and, more specifically, that the kids "want to play more competitive games." I don't hear that nearly as often from the kids.

Why not? Part of the reason is that when I'm coaching very young children (say, 2- to 5-year-olds), I try to incorporate as many games into the activity as I can. Later in this chapter we'll talk about tag games and other activities that can help children develop certain skills while they're playing games.

Most sports programs have given in to the parents who think that the only way their children will enjoy sports is if they're competing in full-fledged games or races. Those sport programs provide a plethora of competitive situations for children as young as 4 or 5. My children have all been involved in soccer and hockey programs that offer one practice and one game a week. The downside to such a program is that there aren't enough practices to allow the children to develop their skills so they can succeed in the games.

Those same parents who typically want their children in more competitive situations don't badger their children's piano teacher to let them play a piano recital every week. They realize that in order to play in the recital, their child must practice and develop a certain skill level first. Sports should be exactly the same.

That doesn't mean competitive situations are a bad thing for children. The message I am trying to put forward is that children should be given the opportunity to develop their skills before they get thrown into a game or a race.

It's also important to make sure the children can see how their skills are developing. In the next section, I'll talk about skill development. At this point, I'll simply try to emphasize how important it is to find a program that spends more time developing skills than being competitive.

Coaching Philosophies

I am constantly amazed at how many children stick with programs that provide very little positive encouragement. One year, I was working as an assistant coach with my son's hockey team. I will never forget one of the practices we had after a game that we had lost.

"That was the laziest, sloppiest, and worst performance of your lives," were the coach's opening words to the 6- and 7-year-olds on the ice.

Needless to say, the practice that followed wasn't that great either, which makes me wonder why the kids would continue to come out.

The children were having enough fun, at times, to make being involved in the program worthwhile. That "fun," which would come in the form of a goal or a great play, came frequently enough that the kids would keep coming back in the hopes that they would experience one of those great moments again.

You can't afford to have your child's potential enjoyment of their activity be dependant on the chance that they might succeed in a game or a practice. It simply isn't good enough and not ideal for building self-esteem.

Once again, I'm back to my "positive environment" approach. That positive environment will be created by the coach and sustained by us parents as we praise our children for their successes.

Role Models

Many children will gravitate to sports because of specific role models. After Simon Whitfield won the gold medal at the Olympic Games triathlon in 2000, there was a huge surge in children's triathlon participation in Canada.

While athletic role models are important, the most important role models children will ever have are their parents. Research has shown a positive relationship between active parents and the likelihood of having active offspring. Particularly, active moms have a greater impact on the chance that their children will also be active.

Parents Need to Be Active too!

"Daddy, how come none of my friends come to the track all the time?" my daughter asked me one day. After years of going to the track to watch my wife and me coach and train two or three times a week, it had suddenly occurred to her that she was the only little one at the track all those times.

All three of our children have grown up in an environment in which physical activity is the norm. It is part of the day like sleeping, eating, and brushing your teeth.

Making physical activity a family activity is a great way to set the tone—family hiking, biking, swimming, and nature walks are good examples of how to get the whole family moving.

My wife is a perfect example of how you can, if you decide to make it a priority, fit even high-intensity training into your life. Ever since our youngest child turned 3, she has represented Canada at the ITU Triathlon World Championships, finishing ninth in her age group both times she competed.

Competing at that level, while maintaining a part-time job, taking care of everything around a busy household that includes three active kids, and holding everything together while her journalist husband spends so much time on the road, isn't easy, but her disciplined approach to her training makes all the difference in the world.

So how does she do it? Utilizing every bit of available time is the first step. A few mornings a week, she gets out for an early morning workout before the busy day begins. On the days she's at work, her lunch provides another hour-long time frame to fit in another workout.

It's not easy, but by being extremely organized, and disciplined, she has been able to achieve many of her athletic goals, while at the same time being a good role model for the children.

How to Include Your Kids in Your Own Training

We purchased our first "baby-jogger" when my daughter was old enough to hold her head up unsupported—at about three months. Suddenly we were able to run as a couple again, something we had enjoyed so much before our children were born.

Once junior number two arrived, it didn't take us long before we had a double baby-jogger, so we could continue to run together.

Running strollers are a great way for either one or both parents to get outside and run with the kids. We also purchased a bike seat that we used with the kids when they were very young, which allowed us to do some easy biking.

Once the kids were old enough, we were able to go for a run while they biked along next to us, which ended up being a great workout for everyone involved. Although when the kids are younger, you might find you need to stop a few times … and, of course, you can't go too far!

The kids have also grown up with regular trips to the track, or to a loop close to our house where we do transition workouts. They were always able to keep themselves busy while we did a quick workout—it's amazing how much a long-jump pit resembles a sand box!

It's important for you to keep active as a parent, no matter how busy things get around the house … so use your imagination, be disciplined, and get out there!

Nutrition

As a coach, people I work with often ask me about various new diets they have heard about and want to try. I always ask them one simple question when they ask me about one of these diets—can you see yourself on this diet for the rest of your life?

Proper nutrition, like physical activity, should be part of your lifestyle. It's not something you do for a week or two, then take a few weeks away from.

The lifestyle component of nutrition is even more important for your children. It's critical that we start them off right. The eating habits you help your children develop in their early years has a huge impact on the rest of their lives.

Childhood obesity is a major problem with young children these days. Much of that can be attributed to poor eating habits and physical inactivity. We all know intuitively that we shouldn't be eating foods laden with fat and sugar, yet we often make those kind of food choices because those types of foods are so readily available. In the busy, go-go-go lifestyle so many of us lead, we often make our choices based on convenience rather than our health.

We can't afford to make those choices for our children, though ... especially if we want to enhance their active, sporting lifestyles!

In Canada, we have an amazing nutritional resource that has been put together by the government that offers a reasonable eating guide. It's called "Canada's Food Guide," and it provides appropriate amounts of food from each of the four food groups. A range of serving sizes is provided for each group. Younger children should choose a lower number of servings, while active growing teens would eat the higher number of servings.

The four food groups are:
▲ Grain Products—5-12 servings per day. A serving would include one slice of bread, 30 grams of cereal. Two servings would include a cup (250ml) of pasta or rice.
▲ Vegetables and Fruit—5-10 servings per day. A serving would include a medium size vegetable or fruit, or a cup of salad.

▲ Milk Products—Children 4-9 years old, 2-3 servings per day; Youth 10-16 years, 3-4 servings per day; Adults 2-4 servings per day. A serving includes one cup of milk or two slices (50g) of cheese.

▲ Meat and Alternatives—2-3 servings per day. A serving includes 50-100 grams of meat, poultry or fish, or 2 tablespoons (30ml) of peanut butter.

Starting the day off right with a good breakfast is critical, especially with busy, active children in the house. In the Mackinnon household, we have a simple breakfast rule that gets the day off to a good nutritional start—breakfast needs to include something from at least three different food groups. From there on in, it's much easier to complete the day's quota from each of the food groups.

Moderation is the key to every healthy diet. It's OK to have the occasional bag of potato chips or piece of chocolate. It's when these not-so-healthy choices become a regular occurrence that children can begin to get into trouble.

So much of nutrition comes down to common sense. We all have a pretty good idea of what we should and shouldn't be eating ... it's getting ourselves to follow that common sense that isn't always easy!

As in physical activity, role modeling when it comes to eating is really important. Kids don't miss a thing—and if they see you making poor food choices, they're likely going to follow suit.

Section 2: Active Training

Playing Active Games

If you are able to create a workout group with a number of children, one of the best ways to start each workout is to have the kids play some games. Playing these games is a great way for the kids to get themselves warmed up, but it also helps promote an atmosphere of cooperation and fun within the group.

Done correctly, some games can be a great workout all by themselves, too!

Even if you're only working with your own children, you can incorporate some of these games into your daily "workouts." The obstacle course activity described later in this section is a fun activity no matter how many children are involved!

Tag Games

Simple tag games are a great way to get started with a group of children, especially if your group consists of children under the age of 8.

▲ One person as "it"

This, of course, is the typical tag game that we are all most used to. One person is "it," and chases the rest of the children in the group until such time as he or she can touch another person in the group, who then becomes "it."

Limit the play area for this game depending on the size of the group. I find that this works well for a group up to about 15 or so.

▲ Last man out (group tag)

In this version of our tag game, once you are tagged, you then work with the person who is "it" to catch the rest of the people in the group. The winner—the last person to get caught—then becomes the first person to be "it" in the next game.

▲ British Bulldog

This is a version of group tag played on some sort of a field or court. One person stands in the middle of the field, with all of the children lined up along one end. The person in the middle yells "British Bulldog" and the children have to run from one end of the playing area to the other. The person in the middle tries to touch as many people as possible as they run by. Once caught, the children have to help catch the rest of the group as they run by.

This game can be modified to create a great workout by putting a time limit for the run from one side of the field to the other. Suddenly, the run back and forth becomes a timed interval!

▲ Parents chase the kids, kids chase the parents

With really young children, having them chase mom and dad can be a fun way to start the "workout." This is a great way to keep the parents involved with the group, too. After a couple of minutes, switch things around, and have the parents chase the kids around.

Ball Games

▲ Frisbee Football ... with a football

One of my favourite ball games with children follows the rules of "ultimate Frisbee" or "Frisbee football," but rather than using a Frisbee, we use a ball.

The group is split into two teams. The object of the game is to get the ball past the opposing team's goal line. The children pass the ball to their team-mates, but aren't allowed to move when they're holding the ball.

The opposing team tries to intercept passes, or to simply knock the ball down during a pass. If the ball is dropped, it then goes to the other team.

This is a great game for teaching children how to move "without" the ball, an important skill in such sports as soccer, basketball or hockey.

One way to ensure that everyone has a chance to touch the ball is to add a rule that the entire team must touch the ball at least once before a "goal" can be scored.

▲ Other ball games

A quick game of soccer, if your activity is based outside, or a game of basketball, if you're using a gymnasium, can also be a fun way to keep the kids occupied for a few minutes during a practice.

Be careful that these games don't become dominated by a few superstars who relegate the rest of the group to spectators.

Relay Competitions

Kids love to race, so adding some relay competitions to your activity can be a great way to add some fun to the day. You can divide the group into as many teams as you can (I like to have teams of at least three). The smaller the group, the less rest time the children will have, which enhances the workout they will get during the activity.

▲ Out and back relay

Starting with a simple run of 10- to 15-meters is a great way to get things moving. Set up a series of cones and have the kids run around the cone and run back to tag the next person in their group.

This type of relay can also be done around a loop.

▲ Back and forth relay

In this version of the relay, the interval needs to be longer—usually about 50 meters or so. Two team members line up on one side, one lines up on the other. The first runner runs to the second runner. The second runner runs straight back to the third runner, who runs straight back to tag the first runner again.

This relay can be a tough one—the kids don't have much recovery time in between each run!

Do a set like this for about two or three minutes, then have the kids take a short break before repeating the relay again.

▲ Calisthenic relay

Here, the children will run to a cone set up about 10 meters away, do some sort of an exercise, then run back to tag the next member of their team.

Some of the exercises you can do (I usually suggest five to 10 depending on the age) are push ups, sit ups or abdominal curls, or jumping jacks.

▲ Crab-walk relay

This time, the cone is set up no more than 5 meters away, and the children walk on their hands and feet around the cone. You can have them complete this relay going forward, backward, or have them do one time of each.

▲ Obstacle courses

One of my favorite activities to play with a group of kids is to set up an obstacle course. Believe it or not, you don't need much equipment in order to create an incredibly fun activity for the kids. Here's an example of an easy-to-set-up course:

▲ Have the kids start by doing "bunny-hops" (both feet together) for about 10 meters.

▲ Then have them run for about 20 meters. Toward the end of the run, set up a small barrier and have the kids jump over that. (Or set up two hoops and have the kids jump from one to the other.)

▲ Find some sort of a bench or narrow piece of wood to balance along.

▲ Designate two 5-meter stretches in which the kids have to hop on one leg only—5 meters on the left followed by 5 meters on the right.

▲ Finish off with a 10-15 meter dash to the finish line.

This is just one suggestion for an obstacle course—let your imagination, and the facilities available to you, help you create your own version!

We especially like to incorporate any activities we might find in a schoolyard playground area, including hand-to-hand walking on the monkey bars and using the slides.

Strength and Flexibility

Strength Training

Children, especially those under the age of 12, shouldn't be doing any weight training at all. Research has shown that strength training at this early age can affect a child's growth and development.

That doesn't mean that children can't do some types of training to enhance their strength. That training should be geared around exercises that utilize the child's own weight—things like push-ups or abdominal curls.

Circuit Training

The hallowed halls of Rugby school in England — the place where C. Webb Ellis "first picked up the ball and ran" way back in 1824 — gave me my first introduction to the world of circuit training.

It was there, every afternoon, immediately after classes and before rugby practice began, that the school's fitness addicts would congregate at the gym for a half-hour circuit session.

This was no circuit for the meek: the goal of the school's physical education teachers, as far as I could tell, was to push those silly enough to try this workout into a state of complete exhaustion. To finish two rounds of Rugby's famous circuit was a feat that few athletes managed.

What could be so hard, you ask? The exact details of the workout have long passed through my memory (the body doesn't care to remember too many painful things), but I remember minute-long intervals of push-ups, sit-ups, dips, rope climbs, box jumps, chin-ups, wind sprints, and balance beam walks. Balance beam walks, you ask? This was so tough, you wonder? All I remember is the fear I felt as I climbed to the beam, which was placed a good 10 feet in the air, and wondering if my exhausted legs and arms would be able to break the fall I was sure I would make.

I never fell, and my three-month stint at England's famous school introduced me to many things. The most enduring, though, has been circuit training.

What makes this form of training so revolutionary is that it is more than just a great workout. Circuit training can be done anywhere, and offers the most time-efficient way to get a workout done.

You probably don't know it, but you have likely done circuit training before. Fitness trails you see in many parks are great examples of a basic circuit. Stations are set up, and you simply run from one to the other doing things like chin ups, push ups, jumps, and abdominal curls — all separated by a short run.

Those fitness trails are possibly the most enjoyable way to do some fun circuit training with your kids, and they will often also include some fun balance-type activities that will help your children develop their athletic skills.

We all don't have access to gyms like the one I worked in at Rugby, but that shouldn't stop you. The only limiting factor for setting up a circuit is your imagination. Some of my best circuits have taken place in hotel rooms, city parks, and my own living room.

My sons and I once did a great circuit while I was working at an event in Barbados. I had only 30 minutes to get my workout in, and the boys joined me at the local cricket pitch for a quick circuit.

After running the half-mile to the field, we started off with a set of push-ups at one end of the field, then we ran across to the other side and did a set of abdominal curls. We did that a few times, then mixed in some other exercises. We did some "Russian splits" paired with chin-ups (for me) and flexed arm-hangs from a bar at the other end. We did some dips paired with full sit-ups.

After going through all that for about 15 minutes, we did some wind sprints across the field. In between, we did a balancing competition on some concrete medians that were next to the park, an exercise that the boys were considerably more competent at than their father!

You can either do a circuit for time or by a certain number of repetitions. Often, I will have the kids work for 30 seconds and recover for 15. Other days, I will have them complete 10 reps of each exercise, and see how long it takes to complete the set.

The best part about circuit training is how you can come up with something different every time you do it. Kids like variety, which is exactly what circuit training is all about!

Things to keep in mind:
▲ Always have the kids warm up and stretch before they start the circuit.
▲ Always err on the side of caution—make sure the exercises you have in mind are safe, and don't allow the children to push themselves too hard. Let them work at their own pace—you should be encouraging, not berating them as they go through the circuit program.
▲ Use an exercise ball to make the exercises more fun. My daughter loves to work on her balance by sitting on an exercise ball for as long as she can without letting her feet or hands touch the ground. You can also have the children use the ball for abdominal curls and other balance activities.

An example of a circuit:
▲ Push ups
▲ Abdominal curls
▲ Dips
▲ Burpees
▲ Push ups
▲ Abdominal Curls
▲ Chair squats
▲ Balance on an exercise ball

Do 30 seconds of each exercise, take 10 seconds recovery. Repeat the set 3-5 times, taking an extra 30 seconds break between exercises.

Glossary of some unfamiliar terms:

Dips: Put your hands on a chair at shoulder width. With your legs straight out in front of you, lower your butt to the ground (but don't rest it there!) by bending your arms so they are bent at 90 degrees at the elbow. Push yourself back up.

Burpees: Start from a standing position, bend down and put your hands on the ground next to your feet. Push your feet straight out behind you so you are in a "push up" position. Bring your feet back under your shoulders, straighten up, and jump in the air. One down, 14 to go!

Squats (Chair): Start standing straight up in front of a chair. Keeping your back straight, bend your knees as if you were sitting down until your butt is almost touching the chair. Straighten up, again keeping your back straight.

Russian Splits: With your left foot in front of your right, bend your knees until your hands are touching the ground. Jump up in the air, straightening your back and switching legs as you go. As you come back to the ground, bend your knees until your hands are touching the ground again. One down ...

Flexibility Training

Any training program must include stretching. The best time to include stretching in any activity is during the warm-up and warm-down part of a workout.

Young children are incredibly flexible. Believe it or not, even we parents were once quite capable of straddling our legs to either side and laying our stomachs on the ground. If you don't continue to work on that flexibility, though, you lose it in a hurry!

Flexibility is a critical component to athletic performance. The stiffer the muscles are, the more likely they are to become injured.

Here are a few key stretches that you should include in your children's training routines to enhance their flexibility:

▲ Hamstrings and Low Back

The "hang-ten" stretch—stand with the feet shoulder width apart, knees slightly bent, and bend at the waist so the hands either touch the ground, or get as close to it as possible.

▲ Quad Stretch

Reach behind the back using the left hand and grab your right foot. Pull straight back to create the stretch in the quadriceps muscles. (The ones in the front of the upper leg.) Do the same with the left leg, using the right hand to grab it.

▲ Calf Stretch

Leaning against a wall, put one foot ahead of the other. Straighten the back leg out to stretch out the calf muscles. (The ones at the back of your lower leg.)

▲ Obliques

With feet a little wider than shoulder width apart, support the right hand on the right knee, straighten the left arm up over the head, and lean to the right side.

▲ Shoulders

Reach the right arm across the body so the hand ends up behind the left shoulder. Grab the right elbow with the left hand to help pull (gently!) the arm a bit further. Repeat the process with the left arm.

▲ Groin

Sitting on the ground, put the feet together in front. Grab the ankles with each hand, and use the forearm to push gently down on the legs.

Each stretch should be held for about 10 to 15 seconds. Never "bounce" during the stretch—make it a smooth, sustained motion.

These are just a few basic stretches. Different sports will often require an emphasis on flexibility in specific areas. When you register your child in a sports program, one of the things you should look for is how much time is spent on stretching and warming up within each workout. If the coaches don't include flexibility in the program, you probably don't want your child involved.

Section 3: Sport-Specific Training

Swimming

Equipment

The equipment needs for swimming are fairly basic: goggles, a swim suit, and a bathing cap.

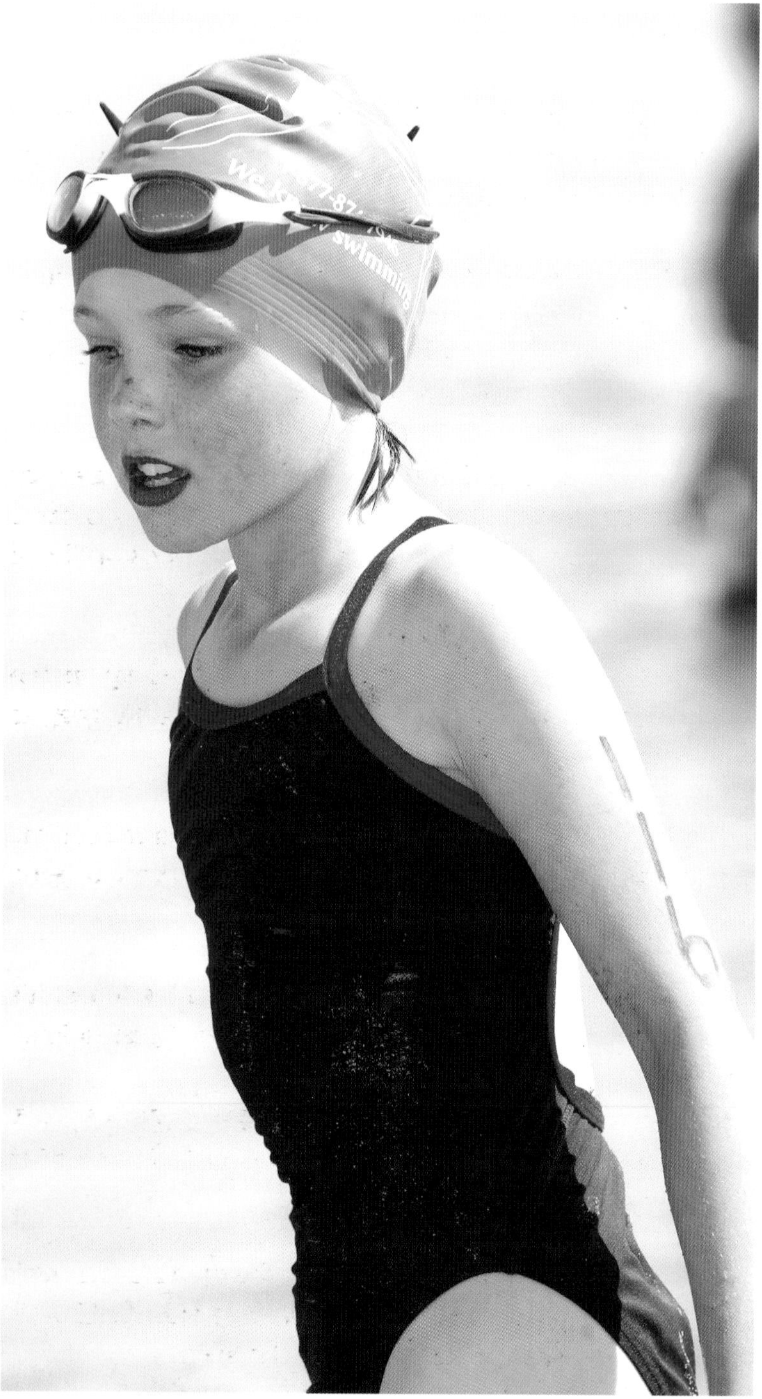

Goggles

Many different companies make a variety of styles of goggles, so finding a comfortable pair that fit properly (read, don't leak!) CAN be done.

That's easy enough to say, I know, and I have seen how difficult it is to put into practice. I have dealt with more than a few tantrums at the pool as pair after pair of goggles were deemed "unusable" by one of the kids!

One of the keys to finding the right pair of goggles for your child is to take them to a store that offers a large selection. Try on a few different styles and brands until you come up with a pair that works.

One of the tricks that we have found to help in the Mackinnon household is to have the child put the goggles on without using the straps.

If you can generate a seal and enough suction to keep the goggles on the face without falling off, there's a good chance you have found a well fitting pair.

If your child will be in the water for extended times, it's worth trying to find a pair that offers "anti-fog" prevention.

Over the past few years, "mask-style" goggles have become available. The Seal Mask for Kids has been a huge hit with my children.

Not only do these goggles fit well, they tend not to leak and also provide a lot of underwater vision, which is especially appreciated during open water swims.

Swim Suits

For younger children, pretty much any swimsuit will do. As the kids become more competitive and interested in the sport, they will want to get a more specialized suit.

"Speedo-style" suits are pretty much the norm in this regard. Made either of nylon or of a lycra/nylon blend, the suits should be snug fitting to reduce drag in the water. Nylon suits aren't as comfortable, but stand up to the rigors of chlorinated pools much better than suits with more lycra in them.

Bathing Caps

For children with longer hair, a bathing cap will likely be required—most pool facilities require caps to be worn by anyone with shoulder-length or longer hair.

Caps are usually made of latex, but there are caps made of both silicon and neoprene, too.

Caps are typically supplied at races and should be worn whenever children are swimming in open water to enhance their visibility. Since so much heat is lost through the head, a cap can help an athlete stay warm in colder water.

Wetsuits

Swimming in colder water is considerably more comfortable with a wetsuit. Since children tend to grow out of just about all their clothes so quickly, this isn't a great investment for children under the age of 12. If the water is cold enough to require the use of a wetsuit, your child probably shouldn't be swimming in it!

Age-Specific Training

How to Start Your Kids in the Pool

All three of my children started swimming in parent-and-tot programs by the time they were six months old. Those programs were invaluable tools to help them become more comfortable in the water.

The more your children are in the water, the more comfortable they are going to be with the process of learning how to swim. In addition to attending any swim classes you might enrol your children in, getting them to a pool or a beach as often as you can will only help the process later on.

Skill Development

As the children grow older, they can begin to participate in more advanced learn to swim programs. These programs are more than sufficient for children between the ages of 3 and 8.

When to Start Training

While regular swimming lessons along with regular trips to the pool are likely enough for most kids to become proficient enough to swim the required distances for a kids' triathlon, children interested in pursuing a more elaborate swim program can certainly do just that.

Be careful, though, before you start your child in a swim program—the burnout in the sport is immense. The younger you start your child in a competitive swim program, the greater the chance that they will be sick of the sport before they become a teenager.

What to Look for in a Swim Program

If you do end up signing your child up on a team, make sure you do your homework before you sign on the dotted line.

Swim programs are notoriously demanding on both children and parents. Two-a-day workouts can quickly become the norm.

At one point in my triathlon career, I swam with an age-group team and worked with a group of young teenagers in what we called the "distance" lane.

One 13-year-old I swam with often swam 80 kilometers in a week! To this day, I find it crazy that this girl was swimming as much as I was running every week ... and I was making a living from my training!

Before you get involved with a swim program, talk to the coaches and some of the parents who have children in the program. Take in a few of the practices.

Are the children having fun? Are the coaches supportive? Do they stress the long-term development of the athlete?

Especially for children under 12, you should look for a program that emphasizes quality training and skill development over extreme distance training. Children that age shouldn't be swimming every day, either.

Swimming Skills

The basic stroke used in triathlons is "freestyle, or front crawl." One arm extends in front of the body. The hand enters the water first—leading with the thumb and fingers. Once the hand has entered, the arm continues to extend under the water until it is straight out in front.

This extension will help generate the roll required for good freestyle technique. This roll involves the whole body—other than the head.

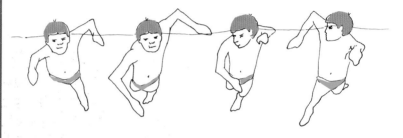

Once the arm is fully extended out in front, it starts to pull under the water. The arm bends slightly as the hand makes a gradual "S" shape under the body. The hand makes a slight "outsweep" out in front of the shoulders, followed by a move inward as the hand comes under the body, and finishes with another "outsweep" motion to finish the stroke. It's important to remember that the hand shouldn't ever cross the mid-line of the body. The elbow shouldn't bend too much, either, during this pulling phase— depending on the athlete's strength, the bend in the elbow during this part of the stroke will be anywhere from 45- to 90-degrees.

After sweeping away from the body to finish the stroke, the arm recovers above the water, preparing to enter the water and start the stroke again. The more the athlete rolls, the easier this recovery phase will be, as the shoulder will be further out of the water. The elbow should be fairly high during this phase, and the forearm and wrist should be very relaxed and loose.

Here are some coaching tips that will help you work with your children on the front crawl:

Head Position

The head should be in a relaxed position, looking at the bottom of the pool. The water line should be at about the hairline, or swim-cap line. The head should remain in that position unless a breath is taken.

Breathing

Speaking of taking a breath, one of the hardest parts of the freestyle stroke is coordinating the breathing action. The head should rotate along with the shoulders when taking a breath. These days most kids learn right from the start to "bilateral" breath, meaning that they breathe on alternate sides, which is very useful and important because it promotes a more balanced stroke.

Kicking

It's important to kick from the hips, as opposed to bending the knees too much. (If you kick from the knees, you can actually generate more of a backward force than frontward!) It's also important to make the kicking motion more of a downward action as opposed to upward.

Triathletes shouldn't overkick—the idea is to kick just enough to keep the legs up, but not so much that the legs will be tired for the bike and run portions of the event!

With that in mind, the ideal kick for young triathletes to learn is what we call a "two-beat" kick: the right leg kicks downward as the left arm enters the water, and the left leg kicks downward as the right arm enters the water.

Hand Entry

The hand must enter the water at shoulder width, with the thumb being the first point of entry.

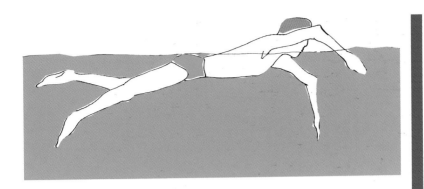

If the entry takes place within the shoulders, a "fishtail-type" motion will develop, rather than the desired roll motion. The hand should not cross the mid-line of the body on entry.

Arm Bend

As the arm pulls under the water, the arm should not bend too much. The elbow remains "high" in this position—it should be above the hand as the arm pulls through the water. Don't emphasize the "S" part of the stroke too much other than to promote having the hand move from shoulder width, to underneath the body, to finishing away from the body at the end of the stroke.

Recovery

It's important that the arm be relaxed during the recovery phase. The elbow should be fairly high out of the water.

Head Up Strokes

It's important during open water swims to be able to see by doing a head up stroke. This head up swimming requires an extra push down on the water as the arm extends in order to bring the head right up and out of the water in order to be able to look ahead.

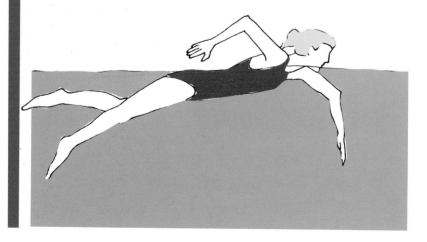

A Seven-Step Teaching Progression

1) Holding a kick board at the bottom, have the child push off the wall of the pool and glide.

2) Still holding the kick board, have the child push off the wall and add a continuous kick.

3) Holding the kick board with one arm, swim lengths on one side. Have the child alternate sides after every 5 meters.

4) On the pool deck, teach proper arm and breathing actions, along with correct head position. Repeat all of these in the shallow end of the pool where the child can stand up.

5) Holding the kick board, have the child stroke alternate arms through the water, using the correct breathing motion.

6) Repeat the above step without a kick board, holding the arm not performing the stroke extended in front of the body.

7) Have the child begin kicking on his or her side with one hand above their head and the other by their side, switching arms every 10 kicks. Gradually shorten the number of kicks between switches until the athlete is swimming a long and slow front crawl stroke.

(From Introduction to Triathlon Coaching, Level 1 Technical, Triathlon Canada, 1999.)

Biking

Equipment

When your children are just starting out, they simply need to ride their bikes. No, it doesn't have to be a "Mackatak Kids Triathlon Bike" (but I wouldn't complain if it was!)—any single-speed bike that fits properly will do.

The important thing for younger children is to simply be active on their bikes. Those bikes need to fit them properly.

Until they are about 8 years of age, it's best to set the children up on a bike so that they can touch the ground with their feet while still sitting on the saddle.

Don't Ride Without a Helmet!

The most important piece of equipment for biking, other than the bike, is a helmet. It must be an approved helmet—in North America that means that it meets either ANSI or Snell standards.

It's also critical that the helmet fits properly. It should be the correct size—there shouldn't be too much movement from side to side or front to back, and the straps should be adjusted properly.

The "V" of the strap on the side of the helmet should be just below the ear. You shouldn't be able to get more than one finger between the chin strap and neck.

Bikes With Gears and Hand-Brakes

You shouldn't invest in a geared bike with hand brakes for your child until you are confident with their bike handling skills.

It takes a fair amount of skill to be able to go from using a "coaster-brake" that requires simply pedalling backward to stop to using hand breaks.

Some children will be able to figure out that process very early, while others might take a bit longer. As a parent, you will know when that time might be.

Racing Bikes

For really serious competitors, there are children's racing bikes on the market. I'll admit—I'm biased when it comes to these types of bikes because I helped design the Mackatak Kids bike by Aquila.

Racing bikes are much lighter and faster than other road or mountain bikes. They have thinner tires, often come with more gears, and are designed for speed rather than function.

You're probably not going to want your son or daughter to take their racing bike down to the corner store on a regular basis, so be prepared to have to purchase a couple of bikes for them.

Here are a few of the features we built into the Mackatak bikes that are worth looking for when buying a child's racing bike:

1. A shorter top-tube so the child won't be too "stretched-out" reaching for the handlebars.

2. Shorter cranks (165mm) promote proper spinning technique and will prevent the possibility of injury.

3. We use a "compact-geometry" design so that the child can grow with the bike—as the seat height is raised, the effective top-tube length becomes longer. The other advantage of this type of geometry is that the sloping top tube allows for excellent stand over clearance—providing added safety.

4. Pedals with "Rat Traps"—an excellent way for children to learn to pedal properly and safely! We'll talk more about that later in this chapter.

5. Solid components. For the Mackatak bike, we chose Shimano's Sora components, which are solid and dependable. In the end, this brings the price of the bike up, but because we chose to provide an upgraded component package, the bikes tend to last a bit longer and have a much better resale value.

Does your child NEED a racing bike? Until they are 10, they probably don't need one. If a child does get serious about the sport, though, they will find themselves frustrated in competitive situations because a mountain or regular bike can't compete with the faster racing bikes some of the children will use in the events.

If you have a child who is eager to compete, and you can afford a racing bike, it will make a huge difference for them.

Age-Specific Training

No matter what age your children are, there are a lot of skills that you should teach them to ensure they will be safe while riding their bikes.

Children will work their way through a progression of bikes. They'll start with a tricycle, then ride a two-wheeler with training wheels and finally attain the balance to ride that two-wheeler without those training wheels.

How to Start Your Kids on a "Two-Wheeler"

I can still remember the day I figured out how to balance on my bike. My father had taken off my training wheels. He held onto the back of my saddle with my bike perched at the end of our driveway and let me get set up and ready to ride.

When I had my feet on the pedals, he pushed me along, and off I went.

After looping around the block for I don't know how long, I finally stopped—thrilled at the fact that I finally was able to ride my bike without those pesky "training wheels."

All three of our children managed to master this step at a fairly young age—two managed to figure it all out by the time they were 3, the other at 4.

Our first clue that they were ready to get rid of their training wheels was watching them on their bikes and seeing how they spent more and more time with the bike straight up, barely using the training wheels on either side.

The next step was to raise the training wheels up a little further from the ground, which encouraged the kids to work on that balance even more.

Finally, we removed the training wheels altogether and took the kids over to the local schoolyard, which had a hard-packed dirt play area. Then came the fun part— running next to each child as they excitedly rode around the park.

Skill Development

Once your children have mastered riding a bike with two wheels, it's your responsibility to teach them how to ride their bike safely.

Going through some of the following drills in an empty schoolyard is a great starting point.

Braking Drills

Have the kids come to a stop at a specific spot. Once they can do that easily, then have them practice coming to a stop and balancing for a second or two before they put their feet on the ground.

Balance Drills

Have the kids come to a stop, and then balance for as long as they can before either putting their feet to the ground or starting to ride again.

Steering Drills

Use some cones or water bottles to set up a slalom course for the children to ride through. As they get more proficient, you can move the cones closer together.

Another great way to practice this drill is to take the kids to an empty parking lot and have them ride through the parking lines.

Have them start by going through every second spot, then, as their balance improves, have them go around every line.

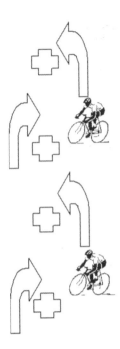

Advanced Balance Drills

Once your child has become very proficient at the balance and steering drills, you can have them try to pick up an object as they ride by it.

You can start by having them try to pick up a water bottle sitting on a stool. Then move the water bottle to the ground.

When to Start Training

For children under the age of 10, training on the bike should simply consist of fun rides with their parents.

Our children did a lot of their cycling while their active parents managed to fit a run into their busy schedules. You have no idea how excited we were when our youngest got to the point where he could ride 8 to 10 kilometers!

How Far is Too Far?

It's important that you, as a parent, gauge your children's ability to handle the distance rides you are taking them on. Make sure they're finishing their rides feeling good ... not exhausted!

Pedals

As your child becomes more proficient on their bicycle, you can have them start to use toe-clips (sometimes referred to as "rat-traps"), which will help them learn to pedal properly. Your child will have to have some very developed bike skills to be able to use these, so don't push this process too early on!

Toe-clips are screwed onto the pedals and have a strap that can be tightened around the shoe. Even with the straps left very loose, getting a foot into or out of the toe-clips while the bike is moving is a tricky endeavor!

Without toe-clips, all your children can do when it comes to pedalling their bike is push down. With toe-clips, they can learn to add another dimension to the pedalling action, pulling up with one foot while the other pushes down.

Toe-clips will enhance performance appreciably, but should only be used once your child has displayed enough cycling proficiency to master them properly.

Note: *Children under the age of 13 aren't allowed to use clipless pedals in competition, which is why I have chosen not to talk about their use in this book.*

Running

Equipment

What to Start With

When they are first getting started, children can, and should, wear whatever running shoes are available to them. The most important thing about the activity is to simply get your child in an open area and let them run!

Once your child does get a little more serious about the sport, it becomes worthwhile to invest in a more specific running shoe.

What Makes a Running Shoe Good for Running?

Shoes designed for running will be more flexible than, say, a basketball or a tennis shoe. That "flex" in the shoe allows the foot to roll after the heel hits the ground before the "take-off" point from the toes.

Running shoes won't have the same lateral, or side-to-side, stiffness that you'll find in a tennis or basketball shoe because, for the most part, the running motion doesn't require that kind of protection. The shoes can be a little lighter and provide more protection where it's needed.

How Long Will a Pair of Shoes Last?

Most running shoes today have amazing soles. The rubber compounds used on the bottom of shoes are incredibly durable. For the most part, what wears out in a pair of shoes is the "mid-sole"—the material between the sole and the upper that provides all the cushioning in the shoe. After repeated pounding, that mid-sole typically "flattens-out", and the shoe won't provide as much cushioning as it once did.

When you run on a shoe that has lost its midsole cushioning, you'll start to feel it. Your knees will ache, you might find you're starting to run into problems with plantar fasciitis. Often people will complain of pain in their lower back because of the increased shock of each landing, which is radiating up their leg.

With adults, the midsole of a shoe is typically good for about three to six months, depending on how much running you do. Younger children, typically, won't be affected by the wearing out of the mid-sole of a shoe — they simply outgrow them!

Older children and teenagers might definitely wear out a pair of shoes before they have outgrown them. When they do, bite the bullet and get them another pair. Get them to use the old pair as "walking-around" shoes until they either outgrow them, or manage to really wear them out!

Racing Shoes (Spikes and Racing Flats) for Kids

As your children get more serious about the sport and begin to compete, the next step, in terms of equipment, is to invest in a pair of racing shoes.

For children competing in track events, that means getting a pair of spikes.

Spikes are very light shoes with "spikes" underneath the toes and arch of the foot to provide more grip and traction when running on a track.

Just about every shoe company makes various types of racing flats and spikes. Like regular training shoes, it's critical that you check with a reputable running store that will not only fit your child properly, but will suggest the most appropriate shoe for your child's needs.

Age-Specific Training

When to Start Training

Young children love to run around and play games. Encouraging that activity is the first step in developing a young athlete. Remember, your children aren't going to figure out what they want to do in the way of sports until they're much older. The best way you can help them to excel in whatever activity they eventually pursue is to promote physical activity for them from an early age.

I like to begin training with kids as young as 4 or 5. At this point, of course, any activities are simply game oriented, but what can be very helpful for children at this age is getting some help with their running form.

It's amazing how unnatural running can be for some children. I find that if you can help the children who aren't as comfortable with their running with their form, they can quickly become more confident in almost any of the physical activities they're involved in.

It amazes me that many coaches will have children work for hours on their form in the pool, but go for years without making a single comment about a child's form while running!

Teaching running form is a critical part of developing a young runner.

Skill Development and Running Drills

When we walk, we're basically leaning forward enough that we're about to fall over, then we catch ourselves, then we lean forward enough that we're about to fall over, then we catch ourselves ... you get the picture.

Running is exactly the same, but we add a bit more momentum to the equation because we add to the "falling over" motion by pushing ourselves forward at the same time.

Here are some "teaching keys" you can work on with a developing young runner:

▲ Arm position:

The arms should be bent at 90 degrees at the elbow. The hands should be lightly cupped—never clenched in a fist or held straight out. Try holding your fingers straight out— you'll see how many tendons and muscles are working hard. That sends lots of blood to those working muscles ... oxygen filled blood that could be going to the legs! A great way to practice that optimal hand position is to carry a couple of small sticks during a run.

When swinging their arms, the children should be encouraged to swing their elbows straight back behind them, with the hands coming close to their hips. One of my favorite "image-tools" to describe this process is that I have the children think about pulling some money out of their pockets every time their hand swings back.

"By the end of the run, you'll be rich!" I tell them.

▲ Forward lean:

The hips should be in front of the foot driving off the ground. The shoulders should be in front of the hips. The whole body should be leaning slightly forward.

▲ Head position:

The head should be relaxed; in a position where as few of the neck muscles are working as possible. I encourage kids to look about 20 meters ahead and to scan with their eyes back to the ground directly in front of them. This way they'll be less likely to drop their head to look directly at the ground in front of them.

Skipping

The first "drill" I ever use with children, regardless of their age (I do this with 4-year-olds, I do this with 12-year-olds), is skipping. The first step is to have the children skip for about 10 or 15 meters. Have them swing their arms naturally.

The next drill is to continue to skip, but this time try going for height. The idea here is to have the children really push off the driving foot into the air. Encourage them to drive the opposite knee up as they push off with the opposite foot.

Once you've done two to four repetitions of skipping for height, the next step is to "go for distance." Now the emphasis goes from pushing straight up off the back foot to pushing along the ground with that back foot. When done correctly, the children will feel the muscles in their upper thighs working.

Mach Drills

After a few weeks of working on the skipping drill, the next step in the drill progression is to begin working on "Mach" drills.

Developed by Canadian sprinting coach Gerard Mach, these drills isolate each part or phase of the running motion, enabling the athlete to develop both skill and strength in each phase.

Each drill should be done walking at first, and then athletes should do them with a skip between each stride.

▲ The "A" drill

The emphasis with the "A" drill is to fully extend the driving leg. As the left leg pushes off the ground, the right leg bends at both the hip and the knee, creating 90 degree angles at both. The right foot is brought straight back to the ground, and then becomes the driving leg while the left leg bends up.

Most children, when doing the "A" drill, will try to bring their knees up too high—the knee only has to get high enough so the upper leg is parallel to the ground.

▲ The "B" drill

The next progression after the "A" drill works on the "pulling-back" motion of the leg into the ground. This is a critical phase in the running stride—the quicker the leg can get back to the ground the faster the runner's turnover will be.

When this is coupled with efficient positioning of the hips (ahead of the drive foot), the runners will not only increase their turnover, but they will increase their stride length because all of their energy will go into moving them forward.

The "B" drill starts in the same way as the "A" drill, but instead of bringing the foot straight back to the ground, the athlete extends the flexed leg forward and then pulls the foot quickly back to the ground.

▲ The "C" drill

This is the easiest of the three Mach drills to master. The "C" drill is simply a "bum-kick!"

This drill is designed to emphasize the recovery phase of the leg, when it bends back and then moves forward. The runners simply lift their legs up behind them, kicking themselves in the behind as they do that.

It's important to stress to the children that they should be swinging their arms correctly (brushing those pockets!) and quickly as they do this drill.

Emphasizing turnover is an essential coaching tool during the "C" drill—I always try to emphasize to the kids that they should have "quick feet."

How Far Is Too Far?

As a race announcer, I am often inspired by some of the impressive performances I see at many events. I am not inspired, though, when I see young children running much further than they should.

These days it's not uncommon for 10-year-olds to compete in 10km events. That distance is far too long for a child that age. While many are capable of completing the distance, doing so only jeopardizes any future they might have in the sport.

Not only are children who run much too far considerably more likely to get injured or "burned out," running too far, too young, can prevent a very talented athlete from reaching his or her true potential.

To compete at the highest levels in any sport, an athlete must have a certain level of "bottom-end" speed. This refers to their ability to run fast. Once you lose your natural speed, it is almost impossible to get it back. Running long distances at a young age tends to affect the ability to run faster once the children grow older.

The kids who complete those long distances at a young age are often the ones who end up being the "pacers" in races—they are the ones who are at the front for most of the race, only to get passed in the closing stages by someone with a faster kick.

"That's OK," you might be saying. "My child isn't ever going to be a world-class runner, so that won't matter."

All I can say to that response is this: Competing with the best in the world requires much more than just talent. It requires a drive and determination that many 10-year-olds who compete in such long races display.

By allowing those children to run so long at such a young age, parents are actually ensuring that their children will never reach the world's elite ranks.

Transition Workouts

Sometimes known as "Brick" workouts, transition workouts are a fun way to practice the transition from biking to running—one of the hardest parts of any triathlon race.

There are a couple of different ways to practice this—you can do one longer bike followed by a run, or you can do a number of shorter bike-to-run sets.

As youngsters, my children used to watch their mom and dad do sets of 2.5km of biking followed by a 400m run loop that we could do right from our house. The kids came up with their own version of a transition workout—bike to one stop sign at the end of the street, ride back, and then run to the stop sign at the other end of the street and run back.

These workouts can also be done by time. The kids can do a three- to five-minute bike followed by a one- to three-minute run. Using your imagination to design some different versions of this workout can be a lot of fun.

In the summer, if you have access to a pool, you can add a swim to the workout. A 100-meter swim followed by a 1km bike and a 400m swim repeated two to three times can be a great set.

During these sets, do your best to encourage the children to follow all of the rules they are going to have to comply with during their races. Make them run out of the "transition area" with their bikes to a designated "mount-dismount" line. Ensure that they put their helmets on properly.

Equipment for Transition Workouts

It's great if you have the ability to set up some bike racks so the kids can "rack" their bikes the same way they will in the race, but it isn't a necessity in order to have a successful transition workout.

Older children who are using cycling shoes will benefit by practicing getting into and out of their cycling and running shoes during this exercise.

Training Routines

So what should a training program look like for a youngster gearing up for their first triathlon?

Here are a few age-specific programs that will offer a reasonable amount of training for children from about 5 to 12 years of age. Remember, though, that for children this age, it's important that they participate in as many sports as possible—they should be active in some other sports along with this training!

Five to Seven Year Old

For children this age, the operative word surrounding their training should be "FUN!" While some children in this age group can handle some impressive distance training, you should be wary of allowing them to go too far in any particular workouts.

Swimming Sets

Children this age should be working on basic swimming techniques. While they can get involved in a competitive program, it's important that the coaches aren't pushing these children too hard.

Once the summer hits, and most of the school year programs have ended, you should try to get into a regular routine of daily activity with children this age, rather than a strict training program.

The summer is also a great time to take in a swim session or two. Most pool facilities will offer two-week programs that provide daily swim lessons for the kids. These are a great way to learn — the daily feedback can do wonders!

Biking

Riding for children this age should be fun and activity-driven, too. You'll be amazed at how far children this age can go on their bikes — my 5-year-old has completed up to two-hour mountain bike rides through the trails!

The key is to let your child work at his or her own pace. Pick a route that offers lots of avenues to head home if someone gets tired. (Sometimes mom or dad might be the limiting factor.) Don't be afraid to take lots of breaks along the way — especially if it's very hot. Make sure you bring some water with you, too.

The one "structured" bike ride you need to include within your biking schedule is some time in a playground or empty parking lot where you can work on some bike handling skills. That should happen at least once a week in the early part of the season and can tail off to the occasional trip as the summer progresses.

Running

Most of the running that children in this age-group should be doing is while they are playing other games. You can have them do a bit more of an "endurance" run during the warm up for some of their other activities.

If you do want to head out for a specific running workout with children this age, here's a suggested program that you can try:

▲ Start with a 3 to 10-minute straight run as a warm-up. Encourage the children to run for the whole time—so they'll have to go out easier than they'll want to!

▲ Then have them run through the stretching routine outlined earlier in the book.

▲ If you have a group of children, have them play some of the active games described earlier in the book, too.

▲ Older children can do some specific running intervals. Pick a distance of 100-200 meters, and have the children do 4 to 6 repeats with a full recovery—meaning they should walk or jog back to the start after they've finished.

▲ Finish off with a few active games and some more stretching.

Eight to Twelve Year Old

A good rule of thumb to follow in terms of training volume is to complete up to twice the goal race distance in a workout. So, if an 8-year-old is expected to complete a 100-meter swim in a race, he or she should build up his or her training so he or she can do up to a 200-meter workout in the pool.

The same holds true for biking and running.

Children in this age group will benefit from some more specific training in each sport, including interval training in all three disciplines. How often they train in each discipline will depend on their fitness level and how involved they are in other sports and activities.

When first starting out, it's probably realistic to aim for one workout a day, with two days off every week to pursue other activities.

Here's a sample schedule for a beginner:

- Monday: Off
- Tuesday: Swim
- Wednesday: Bike
- Thursday: Run
- Friday: Off
- Saturday: Swim
- Sunday: Bike/Run Transition Workout

A more advanced competitor can add another couple of workouts to the program:

- Monday: Off
- Tuesday: Swim (intervals)/Run (easy)
- Wednesday: Bike (intervals)
- Thursday: Swim (easy)/Run (intervals)
- Friday: Off
- Saturday: Swim (intervals)/Bike (easy)
- Sunday: Bike/Run Transition Workout

Here are some suggested training sets for 8- and 9-year-olds:

(*Note: Some of the training below refers to interval training. This requires completing a set distance or time, say one length of a 25-meter pool or one minute of hard cycling, followed by a rest "interval" of a given time.*)

Swimming:

▲ 100 to 200 meter straight swim

▲ 4 x 25m (one length)/15SRI (seconds rest interval); 2 x 50m/30SRI

▲ 8 x 25m/30SRI

▲ Easy workouts should be about goal race distance

Biking:

▲ 5-10km straight ride

▲ 5 minute warm-up; 5 x 1 minute hard/1MRI (minute rest interval); 5 minute warm-down

▲ 10 minute warm-up; 2 x 3 minutes hard/2MRI; 5 minute warm-down

▲ Easy workouts should be about goal race distance

Running

▲ 1-2km straight run

▲ 5 minute warm-up; 4 x 200m run/1:30RI; 5 minute warm-down

▲ 5 minute warm-up; 1 x 400m/3MRI; 2 x 200m/ 1:30RI; 4 x 100m/1MRI; 5 minute warm-down

▲ Easy workouts should be about goal race distance

Here are some suggested training sets for 10- to 12-year-olds:

Swimming:

▲ 400 to 800 meter straight swim

▲ 100-200m warm-up; 4 x 25m/15SRI (seconds rest interval); 4-6 x 50m/30SRI; 100-200m warm-down

▲ 100-200m warm-up; 8-16 x 25m/30SRI; 100-200m warm-down

▲ Easy workouts should be about goal race distance

Biking:

△ 10-20km straight ride

△ 10-15 minute warm-up; 10 x 1 minute hard/1MRI (minute rest interval); 10-15 minute warm-down

△ 15 minute warm-up; 3 x 3 minutes hard/2MRI; 15 minute warm-down

△ 15 minute warm-up; 10-15 minutes at goal race pace; 15 minute warm-down

△ Easy workouts should be about goal race distance

Running

▲ 2-4km straight run

▲ 10 minute warm-up; 4-8 x 200m run/1:30RI; 5 minute warm-down

▲ 10 minute warm-up; 1 x 400m/3MRI; 2 x 200m/ 1:30RI; 4 x 100m/1MRI; 2 x 200m/1:30RI; 1 x 400m; 5 minute warm-down

▲ Easy workouts should be about goal race distance

Section 4: Competition

How to Make Competition Fun

As I've said a few times in this book, we all love to win. One of the best ways to guarantee that your children will enjoy competition is to ensure that they have that "winning" feeling most of the time they enter an event.

Triathlon and other endurance sports provide a great way to engender that feeling and philosophy. As much emphasis needs to be placed on achieving a personal best, or simply finishing a race well as is put on coming over the finish line first.

It's important that, as parents, we remember that fact as we're watching our children compete. Rejoice in their accomplishment, no matter if they're the first or last across the line. No matter what happens out on the course, emphasize the positive things that happened in the race, not the negative.

Skill Development

Until your children have the appropriate skills to succeed, they won't be able to compete well. As I discussed in the first section of the book, I have never been able to figure out how soccer and hockey programs for young children often offer a practice or two and then have the kids start playing games. That process simply allows the natural athletes in the group to excel, while the rest of the children watch the ball or puck go flying by!

Don't put your children in that situation. Make sure they have the appropriate skills to excel before you put them in a competitive environment.

When you emphasize skill development with your children, you also give yourself an easy way to emphasize the positive aspects of an event they might have competed in.

"You had a bit of a challenging time in the water today, but you did much better on the bike, and you managed to really turn your legs over quickly on the run," you might say at the end of a race.

How to Develop a Healthy View About Competition

As an athlete, I have always had a difficult time maintaining a healthy approach to my racing. For some reason, I have always been extremely worried about what everyone else thinks about my racing, rather than simply focusing on my own goals.

In one high school race, I remember thinking to myself: "No one is going to like you if you don't win this race." The pressure I was putting on myself in that situation was immense. That day, I did manage to win, but that certainly wasn't always to be the case. That pressure would follow me for the many years of competition to follow.

To this day, I fight with similar issues while competing—and that's after an eight-year career of racing as a professional!

So how do we help our children avoid similar feelings in competition? The first step is to provide endless encouragement to them. It's also important to talk to them about their expectations going into races. Rather than talk about winning, emphasize the fact that the only person they have any control over during the race is themselves, so that's the only person they have to worry about. Make sure they go into their races with the attitude that as long as they have done their best on that day, they are winners.

Good Sports

I hate announcing at kids' events. Yes, I know it should be fun, but I seem to spend most of my time cringing because of the incredibly insensitive screaming I hear from so many parents.

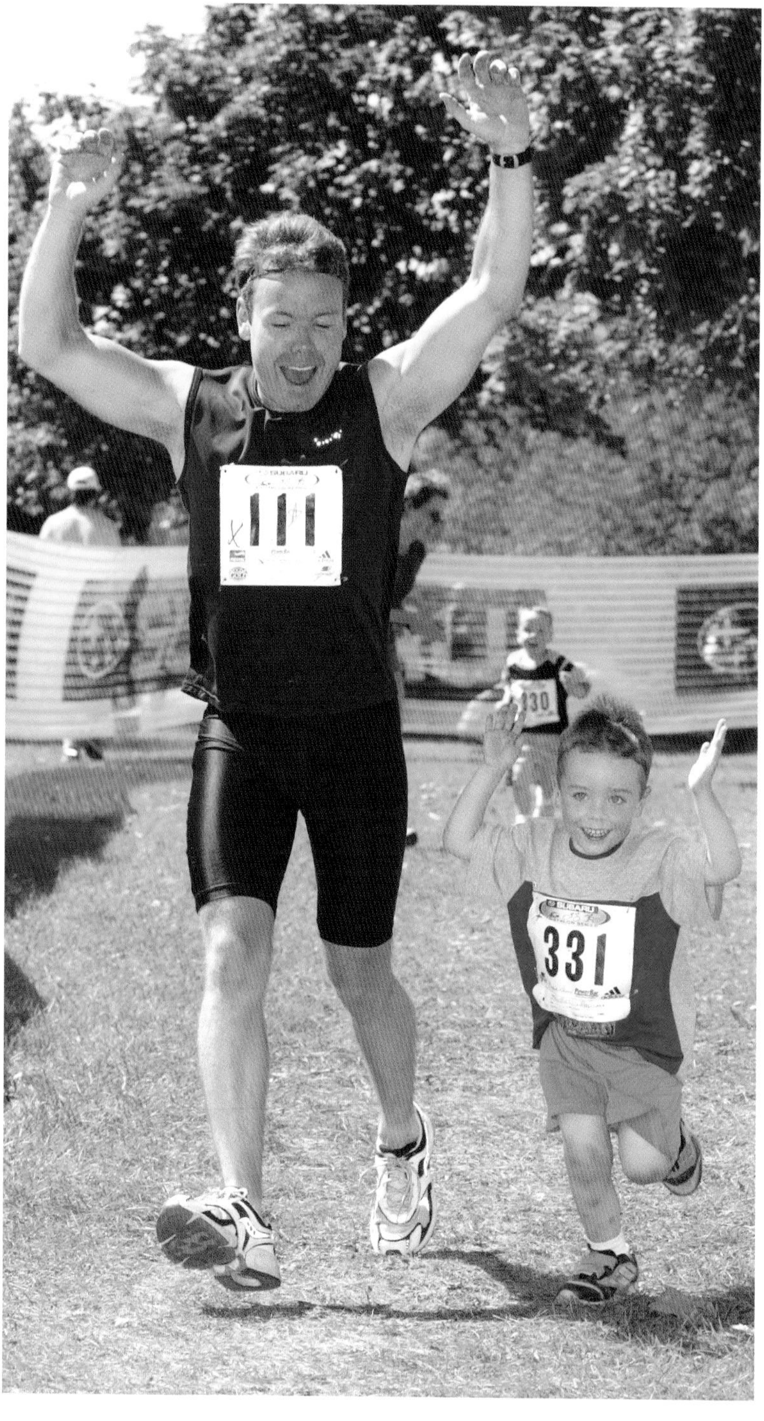
111
SUBARU
331

"Get your butt in gear!"

"You're a minute behind ... run faster!"

"What's wrong with you ... you're not going to win if you don't get moving!"

Typically, I use the PA system to express my dissatisfaction about these comments.

"Yep, we have another "loser" parent screaming at his child here at the finish line," I love to say.

Good sportsmanship starts with good role models. Unfortunately, since so many of our professional sports stars are about as far from good role models as you can get, that responsibility will likely rest on your shoulders.

It's important for you to be positive around competition so that your children can see how it's done. If you're still competing, remember to act appropriately at events and congratulate and applaud the accomplishments of those around you.

While watching races, BE POSITIVE! Not only to your children, but to all of the kids competing in an event.

That positive attitude will rub off, I promise.

Kids Triathlon Events

In Canada and the United States, there are two triathlon series available for children to participate in.

IronKids™ Bread Triathlon Series

The IronKids™ Bread Triathlon Series started in 1985 and since then, more than 40,000 kids have participated.

Children age 7-10 swim 100 meters, cycle 5 km and run 1 km

Children age 11-14 swim 200 meters, cycle 10 km and run 2 km

Relay competitions are also offered.

Every competitor who finishes receives an event T-shirt, an IronKids™ pin, and a swim cap.

You can get more information on the IronKids™ Bread Triathlon Series at **www.ironkids.com**

Kids or Steel™

Many of Canada's premier triathletes, including 2000 Olympic Champion Simon Whitfield, got their introduction to the sport through the Kids of Steel™ Triathlon Series. Each province offers children's triathlon events.

Children age 6 and under swim 50 meters, bike 1.5km and run 500 meters.
Children age 8-9 swim 100m, bike 5km and run 1.5km
Children age 10-11 swim 150m, bike 10km and run 2km
Children age 12-13 swim 300m, bike 15km and run 3km
Children age 14-15 swim 500m, bike 15km and run 4km

You can find more information on the Kids of Steel™ Series through the Triathlon Canada Web site at www.triathloncanada.com

"Splash and Dash" Races

Some adult triathlon events offer swim and run events for children to participate in either before or after the adult races.

These fun "multi-sport" races are a great introduction to the sport.

Other Competitive Opportunities

Years ago, I used to swim with a competitive swim team. One of the kids who swam with the group, Mark Bates, was also a very talented triathlete. As he was finishing high school, he asked me one day if I thought he should quit swimming in order to focus on his triathlon training.

I told him that based on what I saw of the future of the sport—at that time races did not allow drafting on the bike, but that seemed imminent to change as the sport tried to get accepted into the Olympics—he was better off to stick with swimming for a few more years until he had reached a national or international level. I felt that if he was going to be competitive at the Olympic level in triathlon, he was going to need that kind of swimming ability.

Mark didn't take my advice at that time. A few years later, he asked me to coach him, which I did for about five years. He would become a many-time national champion and finished as high as second at Ironman Canada during his incredibly successful career, but he wasn't able to reach one of his goals, qualifying for the Olympics.

While trying to qualify for the Olympic team in 1998, Mark was the one who reminded me of our swimming conversation from almost a decade before ... and acknowledged that part of the reason he didn't fare better in draft legal races was because his swimming, while good, wasn't at a high enough level to compete in Olympic style events.

Mark's story is one I often recount when talking to parents about making sure their children compete in many different sports as they grow up. Competing at the highest levels in another sport, especially swimming, will only enhance a potential triathlon career.

It's important to expose your child to as many different sporting opportunities as possible while they are growing up. Don't allow them to become "one-sport-wonders"—some of the world's greatest athletes grew up competing in many different sports before they pursued one sport exclusively.

Canadian hockey star Wayne Gretzky grew up playing many different sports during the summer—his father used to take his skates away in May and make him play baseball and other sports until the hockey season started up in the fall!

Gretzky would become the greatest hockey player who ever lived, so those summers off certainly didn't hurt!

Triathlon Race Day

All the training preparation your child has done won't help at all without some good organization once you're at the race. Especially when racing in a triathlon, it's important to get to the race early so your child can get set up properly.

It's also important to go through each step of the race with your child. Walk from the swim exit to the transition area with them. Show them exactly where they will have to go when they're leaving on the bike, and also where they'll exit the transition area to start the run.

Your child is likely going to be nervous, so it's important that you remain calm! (You're likely to be pretty nervous, too, but do your best not to show it.)

Remember, it's all supposed to be fun, so do everything to ensure that your children do just that!

Section 5: Appendix

12-Week Training Programs

The following programs provide a more detailed schedule for children as they "train" for either their first race, or a series of races through the summer.

Remember, these are just guidelines! Parents will have to adjust the various workouts based on the child's interest and ability! Also, keep in mind that the most important aspect of any training program for children is that it is fun. Don't hesitate to forget any of the structure inherent within the detailed programs below and simply have some fun being active!

If your choice is an active day of hiking, or heading off to the track ... get the backpack out, and enjoy the day!

12-Week Program for 5- to 7-Year-Olds

▲ WEEKS 1-4:

Day 1:
Swim: 2-4 widths (approximately 10-15 meters) of the pool. Do the widths one at a time, with as much rest as needed in between each one.

Bike: 1 to 2 kilometers (to the pool would be perfect!)

Day 2:
Run: "Workout" as outlined in the running section of the training routine chapter – 4 x 50 meter runs, with a full recovery in between. (Ideally this set is done with a group of children as a relay race!)

Day 3:
Bike: 15-30 minute ride through trails.

Day 4:
Swim: 6 widths (approximately 10-15 meters) of the pool, done two-at-a-time, with as much rest as needed between each set of 2 widths.

Day 5:
Bike/Run Transition workout:
10 minute ride followed by a 3 minute run.

▲ WEEKS 5-8:

Day 1:

Swim: 2 x 1 length of the pool (approximately 25 meters), with as much rest as needed between each length.

Bike: 1 to 2 kilometers (to the pool would be perfect!).

Day 2:

Run: "Workout" as outlined, including 4 x 100 meter runs, with a full recovery in between. (Ideally this set is done with a group of children as a relay race!)

Day 3:

Bike: 2 to 3 kilometer ride through trails.

Day 4:

Swim: 1 x 2 lengths (approximately 50 meters) of the pool. After some "fun time" playing in the deep end, finish the "workout" with 2-4 widths of the pool with a short recovery.

Day 5:

Bike/Run Transition workout:
1 to 2 kilometer ride followed by a 200 to 400 meter run.

▲ WEEKS 9-12:

Day 1:

Swim: 1-2 x 2 lengths (approximately 50 meters) of the pool, with as much rest as needed between each 50 meter effort. After some "fun time" playing in the deep end, finish the "workout" with 2-4 widths of the pool with a short recovery.

Bike: 1 to 2 kilometers (to the pool would be perfect!)

Day 2:

Run: "Workout" as outlined, including 4 x 100 meter runs, with a full recovery in between. (Ideally this set is done with a group of children as a relay race!)

Day 3:

Bike: 2 to 3 kilometer ride through trails.

Day 4:

Swim: 1-2 x 2 lengths (approximately 50 meters) of the pool, with as much rest as needed between each 50 meter effort. After some "fun time" playing in the deep end, finish the "workout" with 2-4 widths of the pool with a short recovery.

Day 5:

Bike/Run Transition workout:
1.5 to 2 kilometer ride followed by a 400 to 600 meter run.

12-Week Program for 8- and 9-Year-Olds

Beginner Program:

▲ **WEEKS 1-3**

Monday:
Off

Tuesday:
Swim: 50 meters (2 lengths) warm-up; 100 meter straight swim (4 lengths without stopping); 50 meters warm-down

Wednesday:
Bike: Easy 3 kilometer ride through trails or on roads

Thursday:
Run: 5 minute warm-up; 4 x 200 meter run/1:30RI (a minute-and-a-half rest in between each interval); 5 minute warm-down

Friday:
Off

Saturday:
Swim: 50 meters warm-up; 4 x 25 meters (one length)/ 30SRI (30 seconds of rest in between each length); 2 x 50 meters (2 lengths)/1MRI (one minute of rest between each interval); 50 meters warm-down

Sunday:
Bike/Run Transition workout:
3 to 4 kilometer bike followed by a 1km run

▲ WEEKS 4-6

Monday:
Off

Tuesday:
Swim: 50 meters (2 lengths) warm-up; 8 x 25 meters (one length)/30SRI; 50 meters warm-down

Wednesday:
Bike: Easy 4 kilometer ride through trails or on roads

Thursday:
Run: Easy 1 kilometer run

Friday:
Off

Saturday:
Swim: 50 meters warm-up; 8 x 25 meters (one length)/ 30SRI; 50 meters warm-down

Sunday:
Bike/Run Transition workout:
2 to 3 sets of a 2 kilometer bike followed by a 500 meter run

▲ WEEKS 7-9

Monday:
Off

Tuesday:
Swim: 50 meters (2 lengths) warm-up; 100 to 150 meter straight swim (4-6 lengths without stopping); 50 meters warm-down

Wednesday:
Bike: 5 minute warm-up; 5-8 x 1 min hard/1MRI (minute rest interval – riding easy for one minute as a recovery!); 5 minute warm-down

Thursday:
Run: 5 minute warm-up; 1 x 400 meter run/3MRI; 2 x 200m/1:30RI; 4 x 100m/1MRI ; 5 minute warm-down

Friday:
Off

Saturday:
Swim: 50 meters warm-up; 6 x 25 meters (one length)/ 30SRI (30 seconds of rest in between each length); 2 x 50 meters (2 lengths)/1MRI (one minute of rest between each interval); 50 meters warm-down

Sunday:
Bike/Run Transition workout:
5 kilometer bike followed by a 1 to 1.5 kilometer run

▲ WEEKS 10-12

Monday:
Off

Tuesday:
Swim: 50 meters (2 lengths) warm-up; 8 x 25 meters (one length)/30SRI; 50 meters warm-down

Wednesday:
Bike: Easy 5 kilometer ride through trails or on roads

Thursday:
Run: Easy 1 to 1.5 kilometer run

Friday:
Off

Saturday:
Swim: 50 meters warm-up; 8 x 25 meters (one length)/ 30SRI ; 50 meters warm-down

Sunday:
Bike/Run Transition workout:
3 sets of a 2 kilometer bike followed by a 500 meter run

Advanced Program:

▲ WEEKS 1-3

Monday:
Bike: Easy 3 kilometer ride through trails or on roads

Tuesday:
Swim: 50 meters (2 lengths) warm-up; 100 meter straight swim (4 lengths without stopping); 50 meters warm-down
Run: Easy 1 kilometer jog

Wednesday:
Bike: 5 minute warm-up; 5 x 1 min hard/1MRI (minute rest interval – riding easy for one minute as a recovery!); 5 minute warm-down

Thursday:
Run: 5 minute warm-up; 4 x 200 meter run/1:30RI (a minute-and-a-half rest in between each interval); 5 minute warm-down
Swim: 50 to 100 meter swim

Friday: Off

Saturday:
Swim: 50 meters warm-up; 4 x 25 meters (one length)/ 30SRI (30 seconds of rest in between each length); 2 x 50 meters (2 lengths)/1MRI (one minute of rest between each interval); 50 meters warm-down

Sunday:
Bike/Run Transition workout:
3 to 4 kilometer bike followed by a 1km run

▲ WEEKS 4-6

Monday:
Bike: Easy 4 kilometer ride through trails or on roads

Tuesday:
Swim: 50 meters (2 lengths) warm-up; 8 x 25 meters (one length)/30SRI; 50 meters warm-down
Run: Easy 1 kilometer run

Wednesday:
Bike: 5 minute warm-up; 2 x 2 min hard/3MRI (minute rest interval – riding easy for three minutes as a recovery!); 5 minute warm-down

Thursday:
Run: 5 minute warm-up; 1 x 400 meter run/3MRI; 2 x 200m/1:30RI; 4 x 100m/1MRI; 5 minute warm-down
Swim: 50 to 100 meter swim

Friday:
Off

Saturday:
Swim: 50 meters warm-up; 8 x 25 meters (one length)/ 30SRI; 50 meters warm-down

Sunday:
Bike/Run Transition workout:
2 to 3 sets of a 2 kilometer bike followed by a 500 meter run

▲ WEEKS 7-9

Monday:

Bike: Easy 5 kilometer ride through trails or on roads

Tuesday:

Swim: 50 meters (2 lengths) warm-up; 100 to 150 meter straight swim (4-6 lengths without stopping); 50 meters warm-down

Run: Easy 1 kilometer run

Wednesday:

Bike: 5 minute warm-up; 5 to 8 x 1 min hard/1MRI (minute rest interval – riding easy for one minute as a recovery!); 5 minute warm-down

Thursday:

Run: 5 minute warm-up; 3 x 400 meter run/1:30RI (a minute-and-a-half rest in between each interval); 5 minute warm-down

Swim: 100 to 150 meter swim

Friday: Off

Saturday:

Swim: 50 meters warm-up; 6 x 25 meters (one length)/ 30SRI (30 seconds of rest in between each length); 2 x 50 meters (2 lengths)/1MRI (one minute of rest between each interval); 50 meters warm-down

Sunday:

Bike/Run Transition workout:
5 kilometer bike followed by a 1 to 1.5 kilometer run

▲ WEEKS 10-12

Monday:
Bike: Easy 5 kilometer ride through trails or on roads

Tuesday:
Swim: 50 meters (2 lengths) warm-up; 8 x 25 meters (one length)/30SRI; 50 meters warm-down
Run: Easy 1 kilometer run

Wednesday:
Bike: 5 minute warm-up; 2 x 3 min hard/2MRI (minute rest interval – riding easy for three minutes as a recovery!); 5 minute warm-down

Thursday:
Run: 5 minute warm-up; 1 x 400 meter run/3MRI; 2 x 200m/1:30RI; 4 x 100m/1MRI; 5 minute warm-down
Swim: 50 to 100 meter swim

Friday:
Off

Saturday:
Swim: 50 meters warm-up; 8 x 25 meters (one length)/ 30SRI; 50 meters warm-down

Sunday:
Bike/Run Transition workout:
3 sets of a 2 kilometer bike followed by a 500 meter run

12-Week Program for 10- and 12-Year-Olds

Beginner Program:

▲ WEEKS 1-3

Monday: Off

Tuesday:
Swim: 50 meters (2 lengths) warm-up; 100 meter straight swim (4 lengths without stopping); 50 meters warm-down

Wednesday:
Bike: Easy 3 to 5 kilometer ride through trails

Thursday:
Run: 5 minute warm-up; 4 x 200 meter run/1:30RI (a minute-and-a-half rest in between each interval); 5 minute warm-down

Friday:
Off

Saturday:
Swim: 50 meters warm-up; 4 x 25 meters (one length)/ 30SRI (30 seconds of rest in between each length); 2 x 50 meters (2 lengths)/1MRI (one minute of rest between each interval); 50 meters warm-down

Sunday:
Bike/Run Transition workout:
4 kilometer bike followed by a 1 kilometer run

▲ WEEKS 4-6

Monday:
Off

Tuesday:
Swim: 50 meters (2 lengths) warm-up; 8 x 25 meters (one length)/30SRI; 50 meters warm-down

Wednesday:
Bike: Easy 5-6 kilometer ride through trails or on roads

Thursday:
Run: Easy 1.5 kilometer run

Friday:
Off

Saturday:
Swim: 50 meters warm-up; 6 x 50 meters (two lengths)/ 30SRI; 50 meters warm-down

Sunday:
Bike/Run Transition workout:
2 to 3 sets of a 3 kilometer bike followed by a 1 kilometer run

▲ WEEKS 7-9

Monday:
Off

Tuesday:
Swim: 50 meters (2 lengths) warm-up; 150 to 200 meter straight swim (6-8 lengths without stopping); 50 meters warm-down

Wednesday:
Bike: 5 minute warm-up; 8-10 x 1 min hard/1MRI (minute rest interval – riding easy for one minute as a recovery!); 5 minute warm-down

Thursday:
Run: 5 minute warm-up; 4 x 400 meter run/1:30RI (a minute-and-a-half rest in between each interval); 5 minute warm-down

Friday:
Off

Saturday:
Swim: 50 meters warm-up; 6 x 25 meters (one length)/ 30SRI (30 seconds of rest in between each length); 3 x 50 meters (2 lengths)/1MRI (one minute of rest between each interval); 50 meters warm-down

Sunday:
Bike/Run Transition workout:
8 kilometer bike followed by a 1 to 1.5 kilometer run

▲ Weeks 10-12

Monday:
Off

Tuesday:
Swim: 50 meters (2 lengths) warm-up; 12 x 25 meters (one length)/30SRI; 50 meters warm-down

Wednesday:
Bike: Easy 8 to 10 kilometer ride through trails or on roads

Thursday:
Run: 5 minute warm-up; 1 x 400 meter run/3MRI; 4 x 200m/1:30RI; 8 x 100m/30SRI; 5 minute warm-down

Friday:
Off

Saturday:
Swim: 50 meters warm-up; 12 x 25 meters (one length)/ 30SRI; 50 meters warm-down

Sunday:
Bike/Run Transition workout:
4 to 5 sets of a 2 kilometer bike followed by a 500 meter run

Advanced Program:

▲ WEEKS 1-3

Monday:
Bike: Easy 5 kilometer ride through trails or on roads

Tuesday:
Swim: 50 meters (2 lengths) warm-up; 200 meter straight swim (4 lengths without stopping); 50 meters warm-down
Run: Easy 1 kilometer run

Wednesday:
Bike: 5 minute warm-up; 8 to 10 x 1 min hard/1MRI (minute rest interval—riding easy for one minute as a recovery!); 5 minute warm-down

Thursday:
Run: 5 minute warm-up; 6 x 200 meter run/1:30RI (a minute-and-a-half rest in between each interval); 5 minute warm-down
Swim: 100 to 200 meter swim

Friday: Off

Saturday:
Swim: 50 meters warm-up; 8 x 25 meters (one length)/ 30SRI (30 seconds of rest in between each length); 2 x 50 meters (2 lengths)/1MRI (one minute of rest between each interval); 50 meters warm-down

Sunday:
Bike/Run Transition workout:
4 to 6 kilometer bike followed by a 1.5 kilometer run

▲ WEEKS 4-6

Monday:
Bike: Easy 6 kilometer ride through trails

Tuesday:
Swim: 50 meters (2 lengths) warm-up; 10 x 25 meters (one length)/30SRI; 50 meters warm-down
Run: Easy 1 kilometer run

Wednesday:
Bike: 5 minute warm-up; 3 x 2 min hard/3MRI (minute rest interval – riding easy for three minutes as a recovery!); 5 minute warm-down

Thursday:
Run: 5 minute warm-up; 1 x 600 meter run/3MRI; 2 x 400m/1:30RI; 3 x 200m/1MRI; 5 minute warm-down
Swim: 200 to 300 meter swim

Friday:
Off

Saturday:
Swim: 50 meters warm-up; 12 x 25 meters (one length)/30SRI; 50 meters warm-down

Sunday:
Bike/Run Transition workout:
2 to 3 sets of a 3 kilometer bike followed by a 1 kilometer run

▲ WEEKS 7-9

Monday:
Bike: Easy 8 kilometer ride through trails

Tuesday:
Swim: 50 meters (2 lengths) warm-up; 200 to 300 meter straight swim (8-12 lengths without stopping); 50 meters warm-down
Run: Easy 1.5 kilometer jog

Wednesday:
Bike: 5 minute warm-up; 5-8 x 1 min hard/1MRI (minute rest interval – riding easy for one minute as a recovery!); 5 minute warm-down

Thursday:
Run: 5 minute warm-up; 4 x 400 meter run/1:30RI (a minute-and-a-half rest in between each interval); 5 minute warm-down
Swim: 200 to 300 meter swim

Friday: Off

Saturday:
Swim: 50 meters warm-up; 8 x 25 meters (one length)/ 15SRI (15 seconds of rest in between each length); 3 x 50 meters (2 lengths)/30SRI (30 seconds of rest between each interval); 50 meters warm-down

Sunday:
Bike/Run Transition workout:
8 kilometer bike followed by a 2 to 3 kilometer run

▲ WEEKS 10-12

Monday:
Bike: Easy 10 kilometer ride through trails

Tuesday:
Swim: 50 meters (2 lengths) warm-up; 6 x 50 meters (two lengths)/30SRI; 50 meters warm-down
Run: Easy 2 to 3 kilometer run

Wednesday:
Bike: 5 minute warm-up; 3 x 2 min hard/3MRI (minute rest interval – riding easy for three minutes as a recovery!); 5 minute warm-down

Thursday:
Run: 5 minute warm-up; 1 x 600 meter run/3MRI; 2 x 400m/1:30RI; 3 x 200m/1MRI ; 5 minute warm-down
Swim: 200 to 300 meter swim

Friday:
Off

Saturday:
Swim: 50 meters warm-up; 12 x 25 meters (one length)/30SRI ; 50 meters warm-down

Sunday:
Bike/Run Transition workout:
2 to 3 sets of a 3 kilometer bike followed by a 1 kilometer run

About the Authors

Kevin Mackinnon has been involved in sports for as long as he can remember. Growing up, sports were pretty much all he ever thought about. At various times during his childhood he competed in:

Swimming, Track and Field, Cross Country Running, Cricket, Rugby, Equestrian competitions, Basketball, Table Tennis, Tennis, Cycling, Water Polo, Soccer, Hockey, American Football, Squash, and Cross-Country and Downhill Skiing.

As a teenager, he was a competitive tennis player – even playing in some professional tournaments. He began coaching tennis at sixteen years of age.

He was a national champion runner while attending university, and after graduating, spent nine years competing as a professional triathlete.

Since the birth of his daughter Chelsea eleven years ago, Kevin has been making a living as a coach and freelance journalist. He writes a "Parenting" column for "City Parent" magazine, and has been a regular contributor to CBC radio and Ironmanlive.com.

Kevin and his wife Sharon, a former track star who now competes as a member of Canada's age-group triathlon team, are proud parents of three children. Chelsea has two younger brothers, Sean and Ian.

The kids love to be active – they love to be outside running, biking, or simply playing! Kevin has coached them in many sports including hockey, soccer, tennis, basketball, track and field, and running.

You can keep up with Kevin's many activities through his website at mackatak.com.

A professional triathlete, **Nicole Van Beurden** recently graduated from the University of Toronto, where she earned a degree in physical education.

Nicole is a natural athlete, having competed in many sports including basketball and track and field to go along with her impressive triathlon credentials. Her "artistic" abilities are demonstrated in the diagrams she has done for the book.

Pictures in the book come courtesy of **Kevin Harrington** from "A Shot-on-Site Photography." You can see more of Kevin's work at a-shotonsite.com

Photo & Illustration Credits

Photos: Kevin Harrington;
                  p. 25 Polar Electro GmbH
Illustrations: Nicole Van Beurden
Coverphoto: spomedis
Coverdesign: Jens Vogelsang

Your Kids...

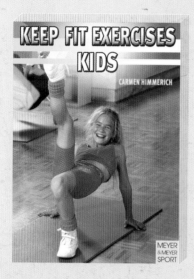

168 pages
Full-color print
100 color photos
Paperback, 5³/₄″ x 8¹/₄″
ISBN 1-84126-150-5
£ 12.95 UK / $ 17.95 US
$ 25.95 CDN / € 16.90

Carmen Himmerich

Keep-Fit Exercises for Kids

The number of postural defects among schoolchildren today is alarming. However, sports lessons in schools are continuously dropping in importance despite this fact.

This book aims to offer assistance to all those people actively involved in putting a stop to postural deficiencies and defects among children and youth in three different steps.

Starting off with an introduction into basic principles, as well as a detailed discussion of the positive effects of gymnastic exercises specifically for schildren and adolescents, there follows a wide variety of easy-to-follow exercises which are clearly explained and illustrated.

MEYER
& MEYER
SPORT

MEYER & MEYER Sport | sales@m-m-sports.com | www.m-m-sports.com

Anz itonkicsS0b/03

...and You

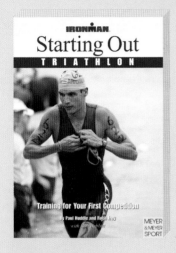

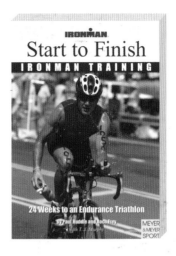

Ironman Edition
Huddle/Frey with Babbitt
Triathlon
– Starting out
Training for Your First Competition

Here's the best book on the market to get you to the starting line. Roch Frey and Paul Huddle are the two most respected names in multi sport coaching. They cover all the bases in the first book of the Ironman Training Series. Besides running, cycling and swimming, you'll find information on everything from weight training to flexibility to nutrition. Don't sit on the sidelines any longer. With Roch and Paul at your side, anyone and everyone can do a triathlon.

160 pages, full-color print
81 photos, 16 tables
Paperback, 5³/₄″ x 8¹/₄″
ISBN: 1-84126-101-7
£ 12.95 UK / $ 17.95 US
$ 25.95 CDN / € 16.90

Ironman Edition
Huddle/Frey with Murphy
Start to Finish
Ironman Training:
24 Weeks to an Endurance Triathlon

Okay, you've finished your first short distance triathlon. Now it's time to up the ante and go further and faster. Paul and Roch are up to the challenge. Longer workouts, balancing work, family and training, adding speed work, recovery and the mental game are all essential when you decide to move up to the Ironman distance. No one has more training or racing experience than Roch and Paul. They will get you to your target race healthy, happy and ready for more.
Guaranteed.

178 pages, full-color print
52 photos, 5 tables
Paperback, 5³/₄″ x 8¹/₄″
ISBN: 1-84126-102-5
£ 12.95 UK / $ 17.95 US
$ 25.95 CDN / € 16.90

MEYER & MEYER Sport | sales@m-m-sports.com | www.m-m-sports.com

MEYER
& MEYER
SPORT

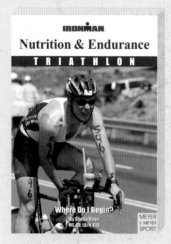

Sheila Dean
Nutrtion & Endurance
Where Do I Begin?

With the busy pace of our modern lifestyle, athletes, whether amateurs or professionals, want the latest information on sports nutrition and they want it NOW! Clearly, what is needed are qualified health professionals who can disseminate scientifically substantiated information on sports nutrition.
This book is a guide to healthy eating for everyone who wants to lead a healthier life. Part one is an introduction to basic nutrition and shows you how to go from eating a poor diet to a healthy diet, while part two transitions the reader into what needs to be done to actually eat for training and competition.

144 pages, full-color print
36 photos, paperback, $5^3/4$" x $8^1/4$"
ISBN 1-84126-105-X
£ 12.95 UK / $ 17.95 US
$ 25.95 CDN / e 16.90

About the edition

The name "Ironman" guarantees for expertise in the field of triathlon and endurance sport. The year 2003 marked the 25th anniversary of this magical event that started with a couple of participants and has now grown to be one of the most popular events and also brand names in sports.

Starting from this anniversary year, Meyer & Meyer Sport is the exclusive publisher for the World Triathlon Corporation with a whole book series, ranging from the best triathlon training to general health and fitness themes.

Renowned authors, Ironman-athletes and legends will guarantee that the spirit of Ironman will come to you in the form of a collection of fascinating books.

MEYER
& MEYER
SPORT

MEYER & MEYER Sport | sales@m-m-sports.com | www.m-m-sports.com

Anz Ironkids 06/03

25 Legendary Years

25 Legendary Years

25 Legendary Years

Bob Babbitt

25 YEARS OF THE IRONMAN TRIATHLON WORLD CHAMPIONSHIP

Ironman Hall of Fame Inductee Bob Babbitt and some of the world's best photographers lovingly share images and stories from what many consider the Toughest Day in Sport, the Ironman Triathlon World Championship.

With a foreword from legendary sportscaster Jim Lampley and an introduction from Ironman creator Commander John Collins, this beautiful book chronicles an event that started out with 15 crazy entrants in 1978 and now, 25 years later, is considered the ultimate goal for athletes worldwide and the ultimate showcase for endurance sports.

2nd, updated edition
Color-photo illustration throughout
200 pages, Hardcover, 10" x 10"
ISBN 1-84126-100-9
£ 19.95 UK / $ 29.95 US
$ 47.95 CDN / € 29.90

Anz Ironkids 06/03

MEYER & MEYER Sport | sales@m-m-sports.com | www.m-m-sports.com

MEYER & MEYER SPORT